CONTRIBUTION TO CHANGE

WILL JONES

Copyright © 2010 by Will Jones

Mentoring M.A.D.E. Men
403 Concepts 21 Circle
Austell, GA 30168

Printed in the United States of America

ISBN: 978-0-578-03749-3

811-54

CONTRIBUTION TO CHANGE

Contents

INTRODUCTION

THIS book was written to be a contribution. After observing people and the environment we live in today, it is painfully obvious that a change needs to be made. In this book I address what I feel that change is. I have identified a few areas that I believe should be an important focus if there is going to be any uplifting or positive progress within the African community. "The African community"—that statement right there might have turned a few people away, but we as people must learn to be honest with ourselves about everything, including the lies and deceptions we've been spoon-fed for generation after generation. Historians and scientists have proven without a doubt that the skeletons of the first human were found in Ethiopia. So if we are descendents of the first two people (the biblical Adam and Eve), and if the remains of the first human were found in Ethiopia, which we know is in Africa, that would make us a part of the African community, not the African American community, not the black community or any other renamed community we have identified ourselves with. Once we as a community begin to properly identify ourselves and quit allowing everything and everyone else in the world to label and define us, then we will be fully prepared to take our rightful place on this earth and in this North American land. This process of destroying our identity has been an ongoing process. It started over four hundred years ago with Africans being taken from their land, being stripped of their heritage and culture, and having their families destroyed. They were forced into a foreign way of thinking, living, and believing that was not their own. This process of destruction continues today, though through a different medium.

Today we are being stripped of our culture and heritage, and our families are being dismantled through music, movies, and the media.

The extremely poor education provided by schools and our interaction with each other, or a lack thereof, is part of the reason we are in our current predicament. We are in a war to save our young men, and the armaments of this war are silent weapons, which include everything from the subpar education they receive to the lack of quality books being used in the classroom. We must understand that anything that has been developed has an infrastructure, a basis, and a foundation; this applies to many things: corporations, buildings, the body, and the government. In order to destroy something in an orderly and organized fashion, you must tear down the top of that infrastructure and work your way down. So in aiming to tear down the infrastructure built to destroy the African community, we must regain control over our minds once again. This book is my contribution to helping the African community in this war. There is definitely a war to save our community, our family, our young boys and girls, and most importantly, our minds. As in any war, everyone has a few roles to play. I believe that writing this book is one of my roles.

The purpose of this book is to spark a flame of awareness in those that may be unaware; it can also be a refresher for someone who is aware but has waned in conviction. There may be someone who reads this and identifies with some of the behaviors that are destroying us but was unable to recognize them as behaviors that are destructive. This book is for anyone and everyone who cares about the positive progress of betterment of the African community. It is for any parent who cares about the destructive paths our youths are on, for any teacher who sees potential in a child that no one else recognizes.

HOW THIS BOOK
IS ORGANIZED

THE book consists of six chapters, with each chapter beginning with a poetic piece that I have written to address many of the issues within our community today. The chapter will then provide a more in-depth look at the issue or concern that was addressed in the poem. This book is in no way meant to offend, disrespect, or upset anyone who reads it. I pray that serious thought is given to the issues addressed and that it does provide a little enjoyment also. I've have been blessed with the ability to effectively put words on paper, and I pray that the words written and the feelings expressed will reach the souls of everyone who reads them and spark a fire . I pray that those who read this become inspired to identify their contribution to change and then act on their inspiration.

Chapter 1

The Recipe

Let *me put you on the happenings in a few of the places I frequent.*

You'll find it's much easier than you think making a juvenile delinquent.

First thing's first: throw away them books; that's right, keep books locked away like his Father and let him run the streets with crooks.

Make it hard to find himself but easy to buy weed and liquor.

Convince him that wearing certain labels on his clothes will make him be a man quicker.

Put him on a track and tell him to run like Flash Gordon, and when the seasons change, Throw him a ball and show him highlights of Michael Jordan.

Imprint in his mind that he started out as a slave, but at best he can be a nigger. Teach him that the most important thing about a woman is her girlish figure.

Better yet, give him reasons to think that every woman besides his mother is a natural bitch, and every time he tries to get his life together distract him with fantasies of being rich.

Don't teach him anything about economics and finance unless it relates to cocaine supply and demand. Keep him disappointed when he tries to do right and things don't go as he planned.

Put him in classes where the teachers couldn't pass the test they're giving. Make him think that having chrome wheels and champagne is the only purpose of living.

Show him gangster movies and porno flicks until he reenacts them over and over again. Make him believe that a small handgun or a big dog can be his only friend,

Keep his head bent in dice games, motivated to win the latest style. Tell him to use his ice grill so often that even he forgets his own smile.

Give him the wrong role model—that is, if you give him any at all. Don't encourage him to rise to the occasion, but to go out in a blaze of glory when he falls.

Persuade him to rebel against the system and "buck," only learning to surrender when he's handcuffed. Teach him that the only way he will ever become a man is if his pockets are stuffed.

Now, I know I've covered a lot of material, and hopefully you understand the sequence. If we keep this up I promise you that we will end up with more than our fair share of juvenile delinquents.

THE recipe is a blueprint for keeping our young males in a mindset of dependence. People learn a lot by visualizing; boys learn to become men by watching men. Because our men are locked away and no one is left to show them how these men lived their lives, our boys are left with no worthy image of what a man does, how a man talks, or how a man acts. A boy can only learn who he is and what he has by being in the company of men. A man who mentors a boy can have a great impact of erasing a young boy's belief that the only way he can be great is if he plays a sport or raps a song. Instead of giving our young boys books to read and movies to watch about Larry Hoover, Ricky Ross, or Frank Lucas, give them books and show them movies about Dr. Cornell West, Geronimo Pratt, Arsenio Hall, and Reginald Lewis. Provide him with role models, mentors, and heroes who are realistic to him and his environment. Don't entertain him with entertainers who benefit from providing entertainment with stories about experiences that he encounters on a daily basis. Give him heroes that are not larger-than-life action figures, but heroes that are just as common as the guy down the street who gets up every day to go to work at a job he hates to support his family.

There is a myth that it is unmanly or uncool to read. We have to kill myths like that quickly. You should incorporate many things into your son's life, and a book or two won't hurt him. Try this experiment: whenever you buy your son a gift, also buy him a book about the gift that you gave him. For example, if you give your son a football as a gift, also give him a book about Ernie Davis or Jim Brown and make it a learning experience for him. Allow your child to select the books he reads; he will most likely select books on topics that are of interest to them. Expose him to environments that enhance his development. One thing that will prove to be great for your son's development is if you begin to identify and focus on his strengths and not his weaknesses. Doing this consistently will prove to help tremendously in building him up. This will develop within him a good sense of confidence, a strong self-image, and a high level of self-esteem. All three of these things have a direct impact on young males and how they will interact within society. Helping young males find, use, and enhance their strengths will be a great asset to them and their successes in life.

Another area of life that I feel we should focus on is to helping young men understand the type of temperament they have. If a child understands his temperament, he can have a plan in regard to how he chooses to respond to situations he will encounter as he goes through life. We can teach our young males that they should be equipped with a variety of temperaments. We can teach them that they don't have to only be calm, or only be aggressive; they can have a balance with their temperament. We also need to help them understand what type of personality they have. This goes hand in hand with focusing on their strengths. If a young male knows and understands that he is an introverted person, he can use his skills and abilities in an environment where his introverted personality will shine. If the introverted child is placed in an environment more conducive to someone who is an extrovert, the child can effectively size up the situation and decide a better plan of attack that focuses on his areas of strength. The choice to focus on strengths and not weaknesses can do wonders for young males.

However, we have to keep one thing in mind, and that is that with any method we choose to use, we must remember that the sole purpose is the better development of our young males, and we should remain consistent in our approach. This characteristic of consistency alone has the ability to lift up our young males, or tear them down.

Consistency, or sometimes the lack thereof, is part of the reason we are in the current predicament. Society has been consistent in the destructive methods they have used on our young males. One example of this consistency is by giving our young males words to use but not providing an adequate meaning of the word. They end up using words in phrases that don't belong, resulting in our young males sounding and looking ignorant. They end up using words that they don't know the meaning of. If they don't understand the capacity of the word they are using, then they're using words that are creating a destiny for them that they don't even realize. Two examples of what I am talking about are the words "shit" and "fuck." Both of these words were originally acronyms. People who transported goods used the acronym SHIT for packages they were transporting, and they placed this acronym on packages that needed to be placed on the top shelves. SHIT means "Ship High in Transit." FUCK was an acronym used by the English police when they were writing their reports, and it means "For Unlawful Carnal Knowledge." In addition, these words are also anecdotal. Fuck has been in the English language since the fifteenth century, and shit comes from the Old English word scite, meaning, "to defecate".

Another way society has been consistent in the destruction of our young males is by glorifying a "gangster" mentality. Making gangster movies and gangster rap popular has played a major role in our youths' destruction. I want you to understand that the word gangster rap is an oxymoron, a big contradiction. Real gangsters are quiet and don't incriminate themselves by talking about what they've done; they move in silence and in the background. On the other hand, rappers do nothing but talk about what they have, what they've done, where they've been and what they are going to do; that's what they get paid for. Our youth constantly see images of shiny things as a representation of success.

These are just a few of the areas where society has been consistent in the destruction of our young males. If we are to regain control of the hearts, minds, and souls of our young males, we have to be consistent in our methods as well. We must consistently provide positive images, positive success stories, and positive interactions with them and others around them. We must model positivity. Show our young males that being on time to everything is cool. Show them that they don't have to fear failure because it builds strength and character.

The fear of failure is another issue that we must consistently address. The issue of fearing to fail is a contribution made to a youth's mind from the evil spirit of abandonment. The issue of abandonment and its effect on the positive development of our young males is illustrated in statistics obtained by the U.S. Bureau of Justice that show that nearly 90 percent of all violent crimes are committed by males who come from single-parent homes, which means at some point in time they were abandoned. The feeling of abandonment makes our young males think that they are a failure, no matter how many times we tell them that it's not their fault that the other person left. This fear of failure will eventually cause our young males to avoid anything that they are not perfect at, which will end up causing them to carry the weight of regret on their shoulders throughout their lives.

We must teach our young males that they shouldn't allow what they cannot do to interfere with what they can do. John Wooden, a great college basketball coach, once said that the team that makes the most mistakes will win the game. This statement is based on the idea that we learn from our mistakes. Mistakes are often a direct result of trying too hard, so if you are not making mistakes, you can assume that you are not trying hard enough; never failing means that you really never do anything. By teaching our young males that failure is okay, we teach them to learn from their mistakes, and the direct result of failure is growth.

I challenge you, as someone who may have a young male around— be it in school, in your home, or in your community—to be consistent in his development, and to help him understand that failure is actually good and not bad. Teach him that life is a beach chair and to not be afraid of dying; only be afraid of not trying. Teach him to reach and walk high, to not be afraid to fall out of the sky. The next time he tells you that he doesn't want to try something new because he's scared to fail, ask him why.

CHAPTER 2

CAPITALISM

Capitalism *breeds capitalists, and this is in everything; if you don't believe me just ask any one of the kings.*

Now, how much do you pay for your monthly insurance policy, and when you switch providers, you're provided coverage inadequately. Listen to me carefully.

The coverage that initially covered you won't provide coverage for what they covered before, and they will drop your coverage if you don't pay what you're covered for.

When you signed the policy, everything was covered under it. Unless a category one, two, three, four, or five hurricane hit, or a flood or an earthquake or any other natural disaster.

When it comes to capitalizing in capitalism, insurance companies are the masters.

We're not even going to address the contradiction of a deductible. Incorporating that into the scheme of things was really a smart hustle.

Pay us once a month, and we will cover you, but if the charges are under this amount, then the bill rests on you.

I've heard that the rich get richer and the poor don't get a thing; that's because the capitalist in this capitalistic society keeps on capitalizing.

You have cites building tourist attractions, the biggest in the southeast, while they maintainthe largest population of people with nowhere to sleep and only food from trash cans to eat.

Bodies stretched across the street sleep, hunger pains rumbling 'cause last week was when they last had something to eat.

They're tearing down projects and building up twenty thousand dollar condos, yet the house across the street is still where crack is sold. Now, this is where the real story gets told.

I need you to listen carefully.

I'm about to expose some facts about coke and crack.

When you're arrested it's not for possession, its because you didn't pay the tax, which is preventing the government from getting its money back.

So you could actually relax if you owned a brick of crack, knowing that you paid the heavily levied tax.

How's that for facts, and marijuana is only illegal because they haven't found a way to place on it a tax.

Now that's capitalism in its truest form.

They say that money is the root of all evil; they also say that money doesn't grow on trees, but I am sure a true capitalist disagrees.

So like I said at the start of this, capitalism breeds capitalists, so if it doesn't make dollars then it doesn't make sense.

"**C**ASH rules everything around me." "Money doesn't grow on trees." "Money is the root of all evil." We have all heard these phrases in our life at some time or another. Money is what makes capitalism move in America and in the world. People are out to get money, and many of them plan to get it by any means necessary. Capitalism, or the result of capitalism, is a sickness, an addiction. It's powerful in its destruction of friendships and even families. Capitalism has caused family members to fight over issues that they shouldn't even be arguing about. A prime example of this is currently going on between Martin Luther King Jr.'s children, and it's about some letters. They are tarnishing the legacy that their parents left because they are unable to resolve monetary issues. Why is it even up for discussion whether they should or should not release personal letters that their father wrote to his wife? The publishing company isn't making things any better; they are threatening to not do a story about Mrs. King because they may be unable to use these personal letters. Now, if the purpose of the book is to honor a great woman, what does it matter if you have personal letters that her husband wrote to her? You honor her by bringing light to the things that she did to contribute to change.

In order to understand capitalism and its power, we have to understand its origin. Before the actual philosophy of capitalism was established, there was a primitive form of the philosophy called mercantilism. The term capitalism was an European Enlightenment term that was used to describe their practices and way of thinking. The earliest forms of capitalism originated in Rome and the Middle East during the early Middle Ages. Now, I wonder, could there be a connection to the Catholic Church and the philosophy of capitalism? Even though mercantilism has been identified as an early European philosophy, the truth is that the Europeans actually learned all about mercantilism from their Islamic neighbors.

Let's look at how capitalism works. Accumulated property is called capital, and the owners of these properties are called capitalists. Capitalism is an individualistic philosophy; in other words it is a selfish, self-centered way of thinking. Capitalism revolves around the idea that every individual is different, so everyone should be free to pursue his or her own interests. Capitalism is supposed to create and establish some form of economic freedom, and this freedom is supposed to be established in this thing called a free market. This thought process is what creates the illusion that within a democratic society, allowing individuals to pursue their own interests will be mutually beneficial to the interests of the individual as well as society as a whole. There lies one major contradiction in the idea of capitalism. How can a philosophy that is individualistic and totally self-centered benefit a group? When we look at capitalism on a deeper level, you realize that you can't run from it; it's everywhere. You see groups that donate billions of dollars to political campaigns so that they can have an inside influence. If capitalism is designed to benefit the people, why are groups so concerned with their individual motives?

Capitalism creates this spirit of separation by detaching people from one another. Capitalism is based on the distribution of goods. Those who consume the goods have no relation to those people that produce the goods. When you eliminate the direct relationship between the producer and the consumer, you're left with only one relationship, and that is the relationship between the consumer and the object that they are consuming. This results in the people defining themselves according to the objects they purchase rather than the objects they produce. This is the exact opposite mind frame of those who are in noncapitalist societies such as tribal societies. Tribal societies are special; they have genuine relationships with the producers of the food that they consume. Capitalism is a tool of manipulation used to control the machine that they call economics. The worldview of the economy is that it is mechanical, meaning that it is subjected to predictable laws. In other words, the behavior of the economy can be predicted, or "rationally calculated," and these calculations are directed toward the future. Based on previous patterns of world events, we can make effective predictions about the future—in theory.

To understand capitalism you must understand that it is based on the idea of progress and that unregulated capitalism produces wealth.

It's supposed to make the natural economy wealthier and more affluent. Apparently that is supposed to explain why the billion-dollar bailout plan only bailed out the people who were responsible for creating the conditions we are in at the present time. You have banks buying banks and the government buying into banks, so you end up with the government not only governing the people, but also governing the money of the people. Controlling capitalism—now that's the work of a real American gangster.

Capitalism creates an extreme form of dependence. As a result of economic collapse, we begin to look at the government and political figures to solve our financial crisis. People become so blinded by their circumstances that they don't see how political leaders use the issues of finance to deceive the public. Why do you think they didn't develop a bailout plan for the people, since that's who is suffering the most, and who they say the plan is supposed to benefit? We must realize that those who are very rich use the system to legally steal from people and society. They do this by appealing to our sense of patriotism. By bailing out the rich, you are not saving the people; you are saving the rich and their businesses. Now the government owns a part of the banks that own our loans and home mortgages. I wonder, why are they closing nonprofit hospitals in the urban areas of New York, but opening nonprofit hospitals in the suburban areas of New York? Sounds like capitalism at work to me.

Capitalism creates the issue of either being nationalized or socialized, and you can be assured that there is a difference between the two. A person who is socialized is a part of a group who decides to turn more of their personal powers over to "Big Brother." When this happens people grow weak and end up needing the powers that created the mess and confusion to help them clean up the mess and confusion. The end result of this is the group being solely dependent on someone else to choose to help them. Capitalism is a universally important concern because we are in a time where we are watching capitalism at work—and it is working in its purest form, which is destruction.

Chapter 3

Process of Transformation

Let us raise our black nation, take these boys we're creating and make them men. Teach them to love, honor, respect, and appreciate women.

Teach them that they are the head and not the tail; you know the boss of it. Teach them that their Godly ordained position is not coming out of the closet.

God purposely provided us the power to provide; we are fathers, sons, brothers, and husbands given the responsibility to decide.

We built countries with our hands from scratch, and monuments linked with the operationof Earth that no machine has been able to match.

We have been stripped of our history so generations to come won't know of our legendary legacy.

Lets take our rightful place in our homes, community, and work industry, and give our culture back what it was stripped of so aggressively.

The men, the strength, the power, the pride we were all stripped of, now we find the tombs holding those qualities up in the strip club

While men leave their wives at home, teaching their sons to do the same even before they're grown. This can't continue to go on.

What happened to each one teach one, and what you didn't know you would allow me to teach our son?

We allow pride to get in the way, though, afraid to look our son in the eye and tell him that daddy doesn't know.

Daddy doesn't know why in school they lie and hide the truth in history books written by crooks suppressing the truth about the land they took.

Daddy doesn't know why they label black as dark and white as light, but Daddy does know that darkness is beautiful, and that everything you see in the light isn't always right.

Daddy will tell you that the true history is hidden, not to always believe what's written, because the truth is what they try to keep us from getting.

Teach him about legends from the past, and how they're truly a blessing. Make sure to provide him understanding of legends living and how they're helping.

Watch your son grow from being a male to a boy and then to a man. Teach him so that on his own two feet he will be able to stand.

THIS is a very strong chapter with a commanding tone. It's an important chapter because it addresses an extremely important area of concern in the African community: growth. We can contribute to change until we are blue in the face, but in order for change to occur, we have to grow. We must grow both individually and collectively. We must grow in our beliefs and in our actions. In our process of transformation, we must address an important aspect of life that we need to regain control over if we are going to achieve progress. The aspect of life that we must regain control over is the mind of the African man. In order to effectively tackle that concern, we have to understand that where we are headed is not where we want to go. Once we have achieved this level of transformation on a larger scale, we will then be able to effectively contribute to change.

The process of transformation involved reestablishing our young males as men, and we do this by teaching them that they are the leaders of their families and communities. For a long time now we have had a large population of males walking around pretending to be men. They even believe themselves that the behavior they exhibit is the correct and proper behavior of a man. In order to fully understand the process of transformation, we must understand the nature of human beings. The true nature of human beings is to be in a continuous state of change—or better yet, transformation. Unlike many other species within our environment, humans are capable of remaining alive before, during, and after their mental, moral and even physical transformation, whereas if certain species don't properly transform, they die. A perfect example of this can be seen in the transformation process of a caterpillar to a butterfly. If for any reason a caterpillar doesn't successfully transform into a butterfly, it dies.

As humans we have the privilege of being able to receive new knowledge, and by having this knowledge we can be transformed. Our transformation is very unique. We are often transformed by where our mind goes, not our body. There are three stages in this process of transformation. We are born male, we transition into being boys, and then after that, with proper guidance and discipline, we become men. I am going to address each of he stages separately, beginning with the mentality of the male. The mentality of the male is controlled by his wants and desires, which are guided by his urges and instincts. When a male is able to release his tension or his urges, he is then satisfied. The male mentality wants what it wants when it wants it. This way of thinking is a direct result of the male and his attempt to receive pleasure.

All of these characteristics that have been identified as male traits contribute to the ultimate handicapping of a male, and that handicap is how he becomes totally dependant. This flaw in the male mentality restricts his ability to take the initiative, and it creates a desire in him to lie around waiting for someone else to satisfy his needs. The male mentality operates in the flesh, and if these are the similar characteristics that others constantly see in you, then you may want to reevaluate your mentality, because you may be in a male mentality. A good analogy that can be used to explain this mind frame is to compare the male mentality to the slave mentality. The slave is passive, is dependent, and waits for his master to meet his needs. One who never escapes this mentality seriously hinders his transformation process. This is just a basic law of human nature. By staying stuck in the state of maleness, the young male remains dependent and complacent. This mentality also transfers to the level of interaction with females. Women, if you are using your "female tactics," such as appealing to his urges and desires as a form of bait, you will only end up catching males, and not men. You must demand something more and stay firm to those demands and expectations. We have a large amount of males masquerading as men, but they are all stuck in a male mentality. Once you've achieved maleness, then and only then will you be ready for boyhood.

The transition into boyhood results from discipline being incorporated in the young male's life. All of the urges and desires that the male exhibits in his behavior are controlled by discipline. A boy initially experiences discipline externally; this comes in the form of someone telling him no . Eventually the discipline comes internally, with him choosing to do (or not to do) something. Discipline assists a boy in developing his reasoning skills. The boy's mentality hasn't learned to respect the order of things, however he has learned that by respecting the order he gets what he wants. This is the time frame when a boy learns to be slick. Providing a boy with discipline actually starts off as a tool of manipulation, and this is due to the fact that his mind hasn't fully developed yet. The boyish mentality is into playing games and having toys. The boy mentality likes to engage in activities that have very little to do with impacting the world. We see images of this boyish mentality in so many of our adult bodies. The brother who always has a game or scheme is exhibiting this boyish mentality. Boys also enjoy their toys. The toys of adult boys include flashy cars, shiny jewelry, and overpriced wardrobes. They get the latest game systems and equip their homes with the newest stereo equipment, and they often get these things before buying their child's school supplies. The adult boy is more concerned with impressing his friends with his newest toys than with anything else.

Here are a few clues to see whether you are a boy. When you have more party space in your home than you have workspace, you are a boy. When you pay more for your liquor than for your food, you are a boy, and when your sole purpose for having a special lady in your life is so she can satisfy your selfish needs, you are definitely operating in a boyish mentality. We are in trouble because the world is full of boys portraying themselves as men. This is especially apparent within the African community. These imitators are the reason why we Africans don't have effective leadership and guidance in our communities and families to assist in changing our current situation. Black-on-black crime is a result of boys pretending to be men. Fatherless children and families is a result of boys pretending to be men. The high levels of teenage pregnancy are a result of boys who were being taught by other boys, who were pretending to be men. Here is a little food for thought: why do you think that those who were responsible for oppressing us found it greatly beneficial to insult us by calling us boys? By calling us "boy," it was a way for them to maintain mental control over us. We must take back the responsibility for our development, which in turn will result in us turning boys into men.

We have all heard that knowledge is power. It is powerful because that's what transforms a boy into being a man. This is why it is important to have a strong, secure support system of men in a child's life: fathers, brothers, teachers, uncles, whomever— these are all good sources of knowledge for the child. They are excellent instruments of guidance that will aid in the proper transition from boyhood to manhood. Men are equipped with a sense of consciousness, which is nothing but awareness, and to be aware means to be able to see things

accurately for what they are. Therefore to properly teach our boys how
to be men, we must allow them to learn how to tackle real-life prob-
lems, and we must observe and watch them find real-life solutions.
This can be done by giving them responsibilities early, be it work,
social, or management. Having responsibility will exercise their mental
muscles of growth and development. As they take on responsibilities,
they will begin to discover their full potential.

Teach your son that his decisions are binding. When he learns
responsibility, he learns to think bigger than himself and beyond
himself. The systematic destruction of the African man started with
placing him in an alienated mind, which was the mind-set of a male or
a boy. Because the mind of a man is powerful, it gives us access to who
we really are. When we understand our manhood, we will know how
to appreciate women and be able to relate to their womanhood. When
we know who we are, and what our true identity is as a man, we won't
continue to contribute to the fatalities that have been destroying us.

This whole process of transformation is about us confronting
ourselves, moving beyond our maleness and boyishness, and standing
strong in our manhood. Writing this book about contributing to
change is my step in taking responsibility to help generate awareness
so that others within the African community can be aware. We must
take responsibility for every child and every adult, because only we can
fix ourselves.

Teach our young males the power they possess. As men they can
change communities, and even the world—but this can only happen if
they change themselves first. Yes, there has been a systematic destruc-
tion of the African race, and this destruction began with destroying the
African man, but we must understand that it didn't destroy our mind,
our soul, the plan that God created us for, or even our ability and
capability to implement that plan. In order to overcome the setback
that we've encountered, we must take responsibility for what's ours.
Know that whatever you can understand, you can be, and whatever
you project, you can become. Males only sightsee, watching reality,
while waiting for a handout. Boys dream and build unreal worlds in

their minds. Men, however, have visions that become a major factor in transforming society, and that is the result of a successful process of transformation.

Chapter 4

Contribution to Change

I'm so mentally inclined that what I write is lyrically underlined as too far ahead of it's time.

We're going to take a ride where many thoughts, feelings, and statements will be expressed, yet in the end there will be only one question left.

I'm a verbal assassin when I'm writing, killing trees as I prove easily that you're not better than me creatively or intellectually.

See, I mentally murder many minds while I creatively devise a plot planning to perfectly place people of poverty in positions of power to survive.

I understand that this is my role to play in this game, but I wonder, have you identified with your contribution to change?

It's time to change what we identify with as what's cool; all these weak rappers with their shallow lyrics are just recreating the fool.

I wonder, what happens when writing withers; what will we want, waiting while we waste time talking to those that think they tell the truth through the daily deception displayed during discussions determining dollars? Our current currency catastrophes create climates causing cheap choice chooser's choices, easilyevaporate every day.

Tell me, why does the NBA draft seem like a modern-day slave trade? The team's master standing on stage calling the next niggas name, while the owner is in the back playing the trade-a-nigga game.

These are the things the untrained eye doesn't see; that's why we started CV20/20 and Thought360.

See, at all times I keep one eye open like CBS, looking at Ted Turner secretly publicizing his corruption on TBS, only exposing my son to some of the stuff on PBS because everything else on TV is just BS.

America has gotten hooked on reality TV; now tell me how much reality can there be when the camera dictates what you see?

I know I took you on a ride of highs and lows; I've even exposed you to some information that not everyone knows.

I told you at the start that I was going to creatively and intelligently exercise your mind, so I hope you've been keeping up this whole time.

We all have our Godly ordained roles to play in this game, so now you can answer the one and only question that remains:

What's your contribution to change?

L ET us get a simplified understanding of contribution to change according to Webster's dictionary. Contribution: to give of time and knowledge, to be an important factor in, and to help the cause. To: used for expression of motion or direction. Change: to make the future course of something to change and proceed on a different course; to transform or convert. So contribution to change is about giving of your personal time and knowledge to transform the African community's current direction. What is it that you can contribute to the positive change within the African community?

I believe that the first step you must take in order to successfully contribute to change is to gain and maintain a full appreciation of your individual self. Love who you are, what you are, and how you were created. You have to appreciate everything about yourself. Stop allowing society to dictate or define beauty. Tell me, why is it that there are some physical characteristics that American society thinks are unattractive and ugly—but in other cultures and societies, those same characteristic are honored, appreciated, and even used to symbolize wealth? One simple example of this is how people of large size in Africa are viewed as wealthy and are high in their socioeconomic status, whereas here in the Western world of the United States, large size is looked down upon as unhealthy and overweight. Who's wrong, who's right?

In this drive to appreciate ourselves, we must learn to be honest with ourselves in regard to where we are in our life, in society, and even in our family and community. We also have to be honest with ourselves about what we do. The things we do are important in our development; what we do is directly affected by the way we think. The way we think controls our actions, and as we all know, people are often judged by their actions. So when addressing our actions, we have to address the issue of receiving improper teachings. We are taught so many lies and are told so many watered-down stories about so many things. One of those huge stories we are lied to about is in reference to where the first upright-walking being was found, and if you didn't know, she was found in Ethiopia, and her name was Lucy. In addition, recent excavation has resulted in an older skeleton of an upright-walking person being found in Ethiopia, and her name is Ardi. So if the remains of the first person were found in Africa, and we all descended from someone, where are we from originally? Great scholars like Dr. Ivan Van Sertima and Chiek Anta Diop dedicated their lives to prove Africans' greatness and the landmarks of development that have been stolen from us.

The most important part in changing this way of thinking is for you to admit and agree that a change is definitely needed. When you make the decision that change is needed, the first change that needs to happen is internally; then it can effectively happen externally. You must own and take responsibility for your individual role in change.

Taking responsibility for your role in change starts with identifying your likes and dislikes, your strengths and weaknesses. Once you properly identify these areas, you can start enhancing and giving attention only to your strengths, which will create a feeling of productivity or progress. Expending your energy only on your strengths will prove to be beneficial for you individually, and to Africans as a people. The Law of Attraction states that the energy that you place into the world will be the same energy returned back to you, so by giving your strengths all of your energy, you make yourself feel good in different ways, and the energy you receive back will make you feel good as well. These other forms of energy will come through other people who share the same feelings, but they are equipped with different skills, abilities, and strengths. The unity that you may establish with these likeminded people will result in the development of a family. It is much better to have a family behind you in war than it is to have an army. An army just fights because they are told to, not necessarily because they all share the same beliefs and feelings. A family is much closer, shares similar beliefs, and fights for many of the same things. It's harder to betray your family than it is to betray a fellow soldier in your army. In developing a family in this war for change, we must establish some consistency, honor, pride, integrity, dedication, and most important, loyalty in all of our relationships. These characteristics will go a long way in establishing a strong bond. These characteristics will help us in readapting the "each one teach one" philosophy in our communities because we will know that we can totally trust the next man or woman to do what is best.

Upon gaining an appreciation for ourselves, we must understand that we are the only ones who can be held accountable for ourselves. We have to stop looking to outside resources to fix our internal problems. Stop looking to someone else to pass legislation on our behalf. We must first admit that America is not our natural land. The constitution was not written for our benefit or our growth. We must admit and understand that the seal in the constitution reflects the actual thinking and ideology of the founding fathers, that the United States of America was to be a nation by white people and for white people, and anybody else that was not white was supposed to be the burden bearers—now, tell me what's united about that? Being a part of this movement of contribution to change is a life-changing choice. We have to be ready and willing to let go of everything before this point and only hold onto the truths about who we are, what we are, and even where we are. A statement made by Dr. Cornell West can best sum up this whole discussion of making a contribution to change: if you really want to effect change in the world, you have to make those things that are now cool uncool because the cool things are the things that are destroying us. So I ask, what is cool to you?

CHAPTER 5

RESURRECTION

What happened to hip-hop?

Can any of you young brothers tell me how it got its start?

We went from songs like "Criminal Minded" to "Snap Ya Fingers Do Ya Step", while we allowed our minds to linger criminally.

We used to take the wackest songs and make them better; nowadays the wackest song is always better.

This blindness has led us to self-destruct.

We generated this culture, so why are we no longer the dictators of its infrastructure?

We've allowed radio and the execs to direct and control our creativity; this will explain why there is a lack of talented rappers lyrically.

What happened to the classic times when knowledge reigned supreme over everyone, while Eric and Parish Made Dollars, Erick B, and Rakim made us clap to it. When Slick Rick and Doug E. Fresh provided the audience with a show, right after Ice-T told us about the Original Gangstas and their Colors.

So I have to wonder where we went wrong and what will it take to get it right.

It's not about east, west, north or south; it's about us using the power of positively speaking with our mouth.

When Kanye graduated, gradually he redirected the misconception of what was cool.

Lupe fed us Food and Liquor, and we still misunderstood and acted like fools.

What is Common to Mos Def—innately—is not common to all the rest.

When you listen to Common and Mos Def lyrically, you understand, and that's what's best.

Now let's be honest with ourselves: when Jada asked why, why didn't we answer, even though we walked around singing it like an anthem?

We lost the Malcolm X of our time because we truly didn't listen—we only heard his rhymes.

A thug to most, but he was a prophet to all, now who's prepared to stand so the order of confusion can fall?

What's your Resurrection?

TO rise again—this is the result we can expect if everyone makes a contribution to change. This poem is dual in nature. The double meaning in this piece referred to our experience in America and our experience in music. In order for us to return to our rightful place, we must once again gain control of our experience. There was a time when individuals such as Martin Luther King Jr., Malcolm X, Huey Newton, and many other strong African leaders spoke out against the injustices that we were experiencing. Yes, I will agree that today we don't have too many strong African leaders in the realm of politics for us to look up to, but throughout time every generation has had musical artists that took on these roles. Some of these artists include Curtis Mayfield, KRS-ONE, Public Enemy, Tupac Shakur, and Lupe Fiasco. All of these artists have shown their dedication and loyalty in assisting in the development of better times.

I am going to tell you a story about two kids who didn't know each other because they lived in different neighborhoods. Their names were Holy Intelligent Person, but all his friends and the other children called him HIP; and Having Omnipresent Power, whom everyone called HOP. HIP was known as the kid who just had to know everything; he was known for his intelligence. HIP was extremely popular and always had the new updated and relevant things. HOP, on the other hand, was very simple; he was a person of movement, and he was always into action. On a cloudy night, just doing the things they always did, they accidentally bumped into each other on the street and started talking. Neither one of them could understand why they hit it off so easily and were just in unison with one another. They didn't fight or question it; they just rode the wave and eventually became a tag team. Whenever you saw one, you saw the other. People even began to speak about the two of them as if they were one referring to them as HIP-HOP, and anyone who knew HIP-HOP knew that those two together were all about intelligent movement. HIP-HOP was about growth, development, love, passion, creativity, and originality in everything they did.

As time passed, HIP-HOP began to receive global recognition for a variety of things, but there was this one particular kid who grew up on the other side of town that just did not like HIP-HOP—in fact he hated HIP-HOP, and his name was Ruthless Angry Person, but everyone who knew him called him RAP. RAP used to sit up late at night drinking forties and smoking weed and working diligently on a plot to kill HIP-HOP. After many years of brainstorming, RAP finally found the perfect plan to destroy HIP-HOP. RAP came up with the brilliant idea to imitate many of the things that HIP-HOP did, but he made sure that everything he imitated would have a negative connotation and result. RAP began to smoke crack and tell everyone that it was the cool thing to do. RAP began to glorify getting shot and how he has shot others, creating an illusion that it is cool to shoot and be shot at. RAP started to degrade our women, glorifying them only if they had big butts, big breasts, and no self-respect. RAP made it cool, common, and acceptable to call our black women—who once lived as queens—bitches and hoes. RAP created this whole world of confusion, and people were unable to tell the difference between RAP and HIP-HOP.

RAP was smart; he took everything into consideration when developing his plan, but he overlooked one minor detail, and that was how HIP-HOP had touched the hearts and souls of those who came in contact with them. RAP fought a good fight for many years, but HIP-HOP has been slowly making its way back to the forefront of the battle lines. RAP never touched the heart, soul, or spirit of the people who listened to him. RAP was focused on being meaningless, destructive, immoral, and downright negative. RAP glorified death, prostitution, murder, drugs, and sex. Whenever RAP spoke, he only spoke about sickness, hatred, and poverty. RAP was all about the bling and any other shiny things he could get at someone else's expense. RAP is the reason why there is a lack of respect for women in society today. RAP continuously created and enhanced many of all the improper and unacceptable images of African women. HIP-HOP, on the other hand, was positive and uplifting to everyone they encountered. HIP-HOP couldn't be bought, wouldn't sell out for the fame and glory. HIP-HOP stayed consistent in their beliefs at all times; HIP-HOP was all about perseverance. Everyone respected HIP-HOP because they only spoke of peace, love, unity, growth, hope, and forward movement. HIP-HOP was real and true.

Hip-Hop and rap—that right there is a major area of focus that someone who wants to contribute to change can address. Music touches the lives of individuals from all walks of life and all different generations. Music is universal, and if what we have been labeling as cool is continuing to destroy us, I believe music is a good avenue to use in addressing that issue. By changing the message in the music that is considered cool, we could possibly have a changing effect on our future. Instead of promoting degrading, immoral, unethical music, we need to start promoting strong, positive, uplifting music that would begin to instill a sense of pride and dignity within the hearts and souls of those listening to it. Having this entity of music stolen from us is just another example of how our heritage, history, and other contributions to the world have been stripped away from us. Africans were the first to walk the earth. Africans created the first refracting laser. Africans created the first productive still mill, and it was an African that created the traffic light. This is what resurrection is about: returning to our original state. Each one teach one. We lost control of something else we created, and the result has been our crucifixion. That crucifixion is a process that is being used to turn Africans into a permanent underclass. Music is just another avenue that this crucifixion is reoccurring.

Many musicians have made contributions to change, and some greater than others. One of the greatest artists that was making a huge contribution to change was Tupac Shakur. He spoke of issues that were sensitive to the controllers of our country, and they didn't want him to discuss them. He was a great man doing legendary things. Thug Life was a movement of positivity, but we were tricked into believing he was a thug. We have to admit to ourselves that he was ahead of his time, because most of us truly didn't understand Tupac the person. He was a family member in this war we're fighting, but ignorance, fear, and hate took him from us. So like I asked before, who's prepared to stand up strong and fight the power so the order of confusion can fall? The destruction of that confusion will be a major contribution to our resurrection, which will assist us in our drive to change.

CHAPTER 6

THE TREATMENT

What if everything in life was the exact opposite of what we know?

What if it was cool to have the latest bling, but the coolest kids in school were the ones who could effectively articulate the thoughts that they're thinking.

What if the rappers we respected, who made it cool to glorify what's illegal, rewrote their rhymes, rapping about topics that would lift our people.

I have a vision about something real far out, in a shack deep in the woods we would sit.

Learning and listening intensely yet enjoyably to the words intellects would spit.

Nas told us it was written, and Common tried to give us the light, but we still refused to seek insight, even when Public Enemy told us the power we had to fight.

Let's take the music back to the time when artists were respected because of their conscious rhymes, and if you tried to glorify crack you weren't pushed out the back, but the front door so everyone would see that you wouldn't be allowed to speak that poison anymore.

I want you to know that women too have a place. Start by teaching her that it is okay to keep a smile on her face.

That she can walk and talk with grace and have good taste. Teach her that her skin is already beautifully made up, but if she chooses to use make-up, use just a little bit for a touch up.

Show her that her self-esteem lies within and that her confidence is not determined by the opinion of men.

Unless that man is her dad, and in that case he'll never have anything to say about her that's bad.

Now, this is where the plot really thickens: where are all the strong black men?

Either in the grave, in the streets, or in jail locked up—and if we're totally honest with ourselves, that's why our current situation is messed up.

We need mentors for both our boys and our men who are dedicated to helping resolve the current predicament we're in so we can keep this cycle from continuing.

Now women, please don't be upset with this truth, but you can't raise your boy to be a man; you can, however, help him in becoming an outstanding citizen.

A man teaches a boy how women are to be respected, and in this our girls learn to accept this and nothing less than.

He teaches him that his position is to provide, not laying around like a lazy leech on his backside.

A man teaches his son not to be afraid of hard work, and how it builds pride, integrity, and character, explaining to him those values and what they are worth.

Help him to learn, know, and understand our history; don't let him believe the true lies his teacher told him in his-story; teach him that it's a contradiction to go out in a blaze of glory.

I'm asking all black men to please stand up; it doesn't matter if you're a degreed professional, a high school drop out, or the local screw up.

Take your rightful place in the front of the line; stop making excuses and start assisting in the development of better times.

There is one simple remedy that can cure our current illness, which has kept us entrapped in our experience in this North American land, and that is to regain full control of the minds of each and every individual black man.

That's the treatment.

I pray that the words written in this chapter hit the hearts and souls of those who read them. Throughout this book I have addressed a variety of issues, but they all have had the same underlining theme, and that is for there to be an effective change for the African community. For this to happen, our men must stand up and take their rightful place. This topic of contributing to change starts in the same place that the systematic destruction of the African community started, and that's with the African man. Families were destroyed because the man was removed from the unit. Man was chosen by God to be the head, the leader, and the provider. History shows us that when you eliminate or kill the head, everything or everyone else crumbles. This is evident in many different aspects of life. One major and important area that this fact is proven is within our families. Men were chosen to be fathers, and only fathers can guide boys to become men of character. By eliminating the man from the family, boys grow up lost and confused, and even angry.

What is a man? I can promise you that if you ask one hundred people that question you will almost get one hundred different answers.

This is because that question doesn't get properly answered when there is no man in the home to answer it for his son. Many people will base their definition of what a man is by what the world would have us to believe what a man is. And based on the world's definition of what a man is, we will continue to walk and address that issue in the dark.

The first thing we must accept in achieving true manhood is to understand, know, and take ownership of the position that men are the leaders of their families. Throughout this book I've been telling you about a war against our youth, against our families, and against our communities, and as in any war, the leader is usually the highest priority. Just like a snake, cut off the head and the body dies. In this war the leader is the man and the body is his family.

In accepting and taking ownership of your position, you must learn, know, and believe that *you are the man God chose to be the father of your children.* God chose you to be in the place you are in with the family that you have. Before you take any further steps, you must acknowledge and accept that truth. Understand that being the leader is not something that perfect men do; it is actually something that perfects men. Owning your position as the head means owning everything that it comes with— the privilege, the power, the responsibility, and the sacrifice. Yes, the sacrifice. With leadership comes the responsibility of knowing when and what to sacrifice. It isn't easy, but a man knows that he may have to sacrifice his own needs in order to effectively meet the needs of his family. Men have a need to feel as if they are involved in something significant in their life, to know that their lives counted for something, and one area that this need can be met is for a them to live a life of serving others.

Once we have accepted and taken ownership of our position, we must model these same responsibilities to our sons. If we don't we will just be creating a monster within him that will eventually make a stage-front appearance. It's been proven that boys who have an absent or disconnected father express anger and pain. They are more likely to exhibit extreme behaviors, addictions, or obsessions, and they will definitely have a sense of loss, a tendency toward indecisiveness, or a lack of direction. Even as men we are a complex mix of extremes. Without a man around to guide a boy through this development, the boy gets lost and frustrated and will begin to lash out in other destructive avenues. Boys look to receive direction from their fathers to find out what should be important to them. Men were created for challenges; it's our responsibility to model for our boys how to overcome setbacks, to stand firm on our beliefs, and to do these things over and over again with each new challenge that the next day brings. The true test of manhood is to demonstrate strength, stability, and the ability to protect and to provide. If no one is around to effectively model this behavior and these responsibilities for the young male, he will continue to journey through life lost and confused, continuously trying to find himself and his purpose. As men and as leaders and fathers, we also play an important role in the successful development in the lives of our daughters. If a young girl consistently watches her father treat every woman with respect, pride, and honor, she will learn that she is supposed to be treated the same way, and she won't subject herself to any inappropriate treatment from anyone else.

You may ask, "Why is it important that our young males learn early to understand and accept their roles as leaders?" Black males have the shortest life expectancy of any other group in this country. Black males are more likely to be killed before they reach the age of thirty. Black males are more likely to die from a drug overdose or to commit suicide. We are the most self-destructive group within society. Our young males have internalized these self-destructive concepts before they even reach ten years of age, and that's because they are consistently fed these images and thoughts throughout their development, making them feel hopeless.

As leaders, as men, it is our responsibility to consistently provide images and fill their minds with thoughts that are the exact opposite of these self-destructive beliefs they currently have. Teach them that this is not the true state of the black man. This is an area where men really begin to shine through. Manhood equals self-definition. Once you can define yourself—once you are secure and confident in whom you are, what you are, and what you say and do—you can feel accomplished in achieving manhood. Men who exhibit these qualities scare those who don't understand it because it is a rare thing. For so long we've allowed ourselves to be defined by everyone else's definition that we began to think that all we are and all we can ever be is what they labeled us. It's a father's job to let the young male know that men define themselves. As leaders, it's our responsibility to control our environment. We have to fix us and stop going to someone else and expecting them to do it. Stop placing the responsibility on doctors, lawyers, judges, teachers, or anyone else. As a leader you teach your son the behaviors that a man exhibits; no one else can do this. The issue of effectively developing men is very serious, because with the lack of leaders in the homes and communities, we currently have boys walking around perpetrating as men. Teenage pregnancy, politics in this country, failing black colleges—all of these are examples of boys pretending to be men. Families wouldn't be becoming extinct if there weren't so many boys pretending to be men.

The issue of boys pretending to be men is another reason that the African community is dying. With boys pretending to be men, our youth have no true images of how a man conducts himself. It's the leader's duty to make sure that the young males under him understand that a man shapes his own character, masters his own will, directs his own life, and creates his own end. I know it seems like a lot—to take your God-ordained position in your home, in your family, and within your community—but that's what leaders do. The qualities needed to succeed are already built within you; you just have to channel in on them and let them shine.

Many lies and deceptions have been told to us in regard to who we are and what we're capable of doing. I want to leave you with this little bit of food for thought: why is it that God's last words in the Old Testament were specifically directed toward fathers, men, the leaders. In Malachi 4:6, God spoke of the resurrection of fathers on earth in connection to the return of the Lord. The Hebrew word for curse in this verse suggests complete annihilation. This to me means that once men start accepting their God-given places as fathers in the home and as leaders in the community, then and only then will man be able to return to the level of greatness we once had. I am going to leave you with three easy and simple steps that will help you unlock your full potential:

1. Look up: Talk to God.
2. Give up: Sacrifice what you are in order to become what God want you to be.
3. Show up: You were put on earth to make a contribution. God has called you to make a difference.

SELECTED BIBLIOGRAPHY

Akbar, N. 1999. *Know Thyself.* Tallahassee, FL: Mind Productions & Associates, Inc.

Akbar, N. 1991. *Visions for Black Men.* Tallahassee, FL: Mind Productions & Associates, Inc.

Johnson, R. 2006. *Better Dads, Stronger Sons.* Grand Rapids, MI: Revell.

Van Sertima, Dr. I. 1976. *They Came Before Columbus.* New York: Random House.

Recommended Readings

The Destruction of Black Civilization, by Chancellor Williams
Breaking the Chains of Psychological Slavery, by Na'im Akbar
Souls of Black Folk, by W. E. B. DuBois
The African Origin of Civilization, by Chiek Anta Diop

ACKNOWLEDGMENTS

W E *are in a state of emergency*, and if you didn't know or don't think so, we need to wake you up. I have so many inspirations for writing this book that I know I am going to forget some people, so please don't take it personally. First and foremost, I want to thank and give all blessings and glory to my heavenly Father, who blessed me with the words and the ability to effectively articulate them during the time I was writing this book. I want to thank all of my family and friends who provided me with the support and guidance that was needed through my journey of life. You all have made a major contribution to my change and development. I want to thank all of the young minds that allowed me to teach and help in directing their lives down the right paths. Many of my thoughts and feelings can be contributed to the teachings and writings of Dr. Na'im Akbar who is a powerful speaker and a powerful man who has dedicated his life to returning the African community back to their natural mind frame. I want to thank Lonnie Lynn, Nasir Jones, Kanye West, Shawn Carter, and Christopher Parker for providing inspirational words poetically placed through their music so I could be able to develop this book. Your songs have been valuable to the betterment of the African community and I thank you. I dedicate this book to my mother; she has always been the support and strength in my life that pushed me to reached my full potential and be the best I can be at whatever I do. Our family endured a major struggle and setback at the hands of many outside forces that were beyond our control, and on July 7, 2009 a force overcame me and my brother that set us out on a path to create, enforce, and establish a foundation of righteousness that would leave a legacy that would ring throughout the world. Contributing to change is an ongoing journey; take it one step at a time and you too will be able to produce change in someone, somewhere, and some point in time. As a product of a nonprofit organization, this book is being donated to many schools in many different cities. If you have come in contact with the information in this book and would like to make a donation to the movement of Contribution To Change or any of its subgroups, Mentoring M.A.D.E. Men, Thought 360, or CV 20/20, please go to our Web site at http://www.contribution2change.com and click on the donate link at the bottom of the page. I thank you for your time and consideration, and I hope that you find what your individual contribution can be and act on it. Because we are in a state of emergency, and without order, there is indeed chaos!

About the Author

AS a graduate from Georgia State University, Will Jones has been working with at-risk youth throughout the metropolitan Atlanta area for over ten years. His journey began while he was an undergraduate student at Morehouse College in Atlanta, Georgia, where he participated in a community service project at a local elementary school. During his time mentoring those students, he realized he had a passion and a God-given gift to be a blessing and a major role model in the lives of many youths. Later, Will worked for group homes, at the department of juvenile justice, and within the public school system, where he had the opportunity to have a positive effect in the lives of many children. Will takes pride in teaching the young males with which he works many different life skills that all young adults should be equipped with. Will realized that many of the avenues that were supposed to be providing rehabilitation, support, and guidance to the children did not display or have a genuine care and love for the children they served. As a result of observing this lack of support for many years, Will decided to develop his own nonprofit outreach behavior modification program, called Mentoring M.A.D.E. Men. Will has dedicated his life to helping the young, adolescent males that many people in the community have given up on. It is Will's desire to see many of the children he has worked with go on to do successful things in their lives. Feel free to view the work being done at Mentoring M.A.D.E. Men by visiting the Web site, www.contribution2change.com.

Mentoring M.A.D.E. Men

For many years my brother and I have been watching our community suffer from the abuse and neglect lead by both Federal and Local government abuse. We realized a few years ago that the only way true change would come, would be when individuals take responsibility for themselves and their immediate surroundings. Recently my brother Willie Jones decided to start a non-profit outreach program (Mentoring M.A.D.E Men). The focus of the program is dedicated to the successful mental, social, emotional and spiritual development of adolescent minority youth; transforming their current state of mind and self-destructive behavior in an attempt to help them realize true knowledge of self. This is our Contribution To Change. For more information about the program please visit www.contribution2change.com. One thing we have realized; people will follow the "Truth", God has given my brother the ability to express those truths in an effective way, and we recognize it is his duty to teach, and to spread truth.

What's your contribution
to change

CPSIA information can be obtained at www.ICGtesting.com
Printed in the USA
239813LV00001B/124/P